T0018088

1000 TRIVIA
QUESTIONS
FOR KIDS

1000 TRIVIA QUESTIONS FOR KIDS

Trivia Questions to Engage All Kids Aged 9-17

TOM TRIFONOFF

Copyright © 2019 by Tom Trifonoff.

ISBN: Softcover   978-1-7960-0479-3
               eBook   978-1-7960-0478-6

All rights reserved. No part of this book may be reproduced or
transmitted in any form or by any means, electronic or mechanical,
including photocopying, recording, or by any information storage and
retrieval system, without permission in writing from the copyright owner.

Any people depicted in stock imagery provided by Getty Images are
models, and such images are being used for illustrative purposes only.
Certain stock imagery © Getty Images.

Print information available on the last page.

Rev. date: 07/25/2019

To order additional copies of this book, contact:
Xlibris
1-800-455-039
www.Xlibris.com.au
Orders@Xlibris.com.au
800427

This book is dedicated to my own children Jenna and Callum for being the best kids any parent could wish for.

And to their mother Carolyn for bringing them up that way.

Never say
"I can't"
Always say
"I'll try"

"The more that you read
The more things you will know,
The more that you learn
The more places you'll go!!"
—Dr Seuss

"Education is the most powerful weapon
Which you can use to change the world"
—Nelson Mandela

INTRODUCTION

At a time when kids are exposed to more information than ever before, how much of it really stays with them and remembered by them for future use? Is information another in the long list of disposable commodities that we need for a certain amount of time and then discard forever when we've finished with it?

Kids can be like sponges when it comes to information and learning about our world-they have the ability to soak up so much, and can hopefully retain a lot of it when they really need to use it. This is where this book **1000 Trivia Questions for Kids** can be very valuable as a way of finding out how much our kids really do know about our world, and beyond.

There are many categories in **1000 Trivia Questions for Kids** that will see how much kids know. Some of those categories include geography, history, maths, entertainment, science, politics, sports, current events and categories that focus on the trivial, eccentric and unusual aspects of our world. There is something in here for everyone, and unlike some quiz books that have specific blocks of categories, **1000 Trivia Questions for Kids** has random questions. It's easy to discourage kids from participating if the questions only deal with one topic. A person not interested in that topic will automatically be put off answering questions about it, whereas if the questions are randomly asked, there is a higher chance of having something for everyone.

1000 Trivia Questions for Kids is an ideal companion for all teachers in the Years 6-10 range. They can pick a block of questions-select specific categories if teaching a specialist subject, or they can just select random questions. The possibilities are endless. Kids can even use the book effectively to fire questions at each other to see how much the other person/people know.

1000 Trivia Questions for Kids has questions that are fun as well as challenging. Some questions have a multiple choice format, some are True/False and most of them are just straight out questions on topics that kids are interested in and can answer confidently.

After the last question in the book are the answers to all 1000 questions. Some answers also provide extra information to the reader. All answers have been checked and are correct at the time of publishing. In current events questions, the names of leaders of countries are correct up to mid-2019.

As a teacher of senior primary students for over 25 years, I feel I have a good understanding of what type of questions students like and will attempt to answer. Students in my classes were engaged with quizzes on either a formal basis comprising teams with answer sheets, answering questions on an individual basis or just having questions fired at them and answering verbally. Every student had the opportunity to be involved, and even the more reluctant ones became engaged after a short while.

1000 Trivia Questions for Kids is dedicated to not only my own kids but to the many students who participated in my quizzes over the years. Whether it was a quiz in a classroom or at a school camp or being in a team that had adults in it as well, this book is for students who challenged themselves and had fun answering the questions. Enjoy the challenge and fun of 1000 **Trivia Questions for Kids.** May each answer that you give be the correct one.

Tom Trifonoff

1000 TRIVIA

QUESTIONS
FOR KIDS

1. Where does the President of the United States live?
2. What are the colours of the Olympic rings?
3. What letter is located between E and T on a computer keyboard?
4. How many cards are there in a complete pack of cards?
5. What is the most popular sport throughout the world?
6. Is hot air lighter or heavier than cold air?
7. In which American city is the Statue of Liberty is located?
8. Global warming is caused by too much of which type of gas?
9. How do you say hello in French?
10. What type of metal makes the strongest magnets?
11. What is the largest Scandinavian country?
12. How many leaves does a shamrock have?
13. What type of gas do plants absorb from the atmosphere?
14. How many strings does a violin have?
15. Which continent is India located in?
16. How many zeros are there in one hundred thousand?
17. Which continent is the Sahara Desert located in?
18. Who sang 'Everything has Changed' with Taylor Swift?
19. Parrots, pelicans and cuckoos are all types of what?
20. Which two colours make up the flag of Spain?
21. Which Disney character has a nose that grows longer every time he tells a lie?
22. True or false: Antarctica is the coldest continent in the world?
23. How many hours are there in two days?
24. Which of the following creatures is not a species of reptile: turtle, spider or lizard?
25. What country is the River Thames in?
26. What two colours are the stripes on the flag of the United States of America?
27. Which of the following best describes the occupation of Captain James Cook: a) Scientist, b) Mathematician, c) Explorer, d) Inventor

28.   What is the largest type of bird in the world?

29.   What happens to water when the temperature is 0°C?

30.   Which ocean separates Africa and Australia: a) Pacific, b) Indian, c) Mediterranean, d) Atlantic

31.   Which sport is associated with a velodrome?

32.   True or false: Jellyfish have no heart or brains?

33.   What is the highest number that can be achieved from rolling a pair of dice?

34.   What name is given to the most central point on a dartboard?

35.   The Empire State Building was the first building in the world to have more than 100 what?

36.   What are the names the four planets that are positioned closest to the Sun?

37.   How many sets of wickets are used in a game of cricket?

38.   Which character is named Jadis in the Chronicles of Narnia?

39.   Which continent is Mexico in?

40.   What is the world's largest rainforest called?

41.   Which ocean is located to the west of South America?

42.   True or false: amphibians are invertebrate animals?

43.   What is the 11th letter of the alphabet?

44.   Which of the following countries is not in Europe: Spain, Greece, Egypt or Belgium?

45.   True or false: the biggest bone in the human body is located in your leg?

46.   What is the largest continent in the world?

47.   How many players are there on a baseball team?

48.   What types of animals only eat plants?

49.   In 2018, which song by Drake reached number one in multiple countries including the UK, US, Canada and Australia?

50.   Which land mammal has the longest tail in the world?

51.   What is the capital of France?

52.   How many bones are there in a human neck: a) 4, b) 7, c) 10?

53.   How many colours are there in a rainbow?

54.   In which continent are the countries Argentina, Brazil and Peru?

55.   Which American singer released an album in 2016 called 'Dangerous Woman'?

56.   Which country do koalas come from?

57.   Berlin is the capital city of which country?

58.   What is the first name of former US President Obama?

59.   Which Hogwarts House does Harry Potter belong to?

60.   What is the 7th letter of the alphabet?

61.   Ottawa is the capital city of which North American country?

62.   What type of shape has five equal sides?

63.   True or False: Our left and right lungs are the same size?

64.   Which planet takes almost 165 Earth years to orbit the sun: a) Jupiter, b) Mars, c) Neptune?

65.   What is the largest ocean in the world?

66.   True or false: Chameleon's have extremely long tongues, sometimes as long as their bodies?

67.   Which of the following letters are vowels: A, F, I, L, O, R?

68.   What do the opposite faces on a standard 6-sided die (dice) add up to?

69.   Which animal has the biggest heart of any living creature on Earth?

70.   Which character from 'The Incredibles 2' movie has the ability to stretch her body into different shapes and forms?

71.   How many ribs does a human body have in total?

72.   Which continent has the most countries?

73.   How many faces does a cube have?

74.   Which ocean lies to the west of Europe?

75.   Which city does Batman live in?

76.   Who starred as Iron Man in the series of films?

77.   What is the capital of Japan?

78.   In which continent are the countries India, Vietnam and Bangladesh located?

79. In what country is the Simpson Desert located?
80. What is the 20th letter of the English alphabet?
81. How many moons does the planet Mars have?
82. What part of the human skeleton protects the brain: a) Rib cage, b) Pelvis, c) Skull
83. In Egypt, the Sphinx is a statue of a man and the body of which animal?
84. Which Roman numeral represents the number 5?
85. Which American male singer released a song in 2017 called 'That's What I Like'?
86. True or false: the temperature around the poles is above freezing for the most of the year?
87. What type of creature is a Bombay Duck: a) Bird, b) Fish, c) Reptile?
88. Which of the following numbers are multiples of 4: a) 26 b) 44, c) 80 d) 58, e) 16?
89. True or false: the closest star to planet Earth is the Sun?
90. Which land mammal has the most teeth: a) Grizzly Bear, b) Hippopotamus, c) Giant Armadillo?
91. What type of food do penguins eat: plants, fruit or fish?
92. Which 2014 movie features a song called 'Everything is Awesome'?
93. What do camels have on their back?
94. Which continent is Tunisia located in?
95. What are the first names of Harry Potter's two best friends?
96. When mixed together, which two colours create brown?
97. What type of vegetable is used to frighten vampires away?
98. What date is Halloween celebrated?
99. What is the first letter of the bottom row on a computer keyboard?
100. Which country won the football World Cup in 2018?
101. What is the name of the system that breaks down food into simple substances?

102. Which major river runs through Egypt?
103. What is the second largest ocean in the world?
104. How many finger holes are there on the front of a recorder?
105. What is the 15th letter of the alphabet?
106. What is the largest mammal in the world?
107. What is a group of lions called?
108. How many players are there in a volleyball team?
109. What are the small orange men in 'Charlie and the Chocolate Factory' known as?
110. Who wrote the play 'Hamlet'?
111. What is the formula for water?
112. How many continents are there in the world?
113. What is the currency of the United Kingdom?
114. What is the atomic symbol for zinc?
115. Which force helps us keep our feet on land?
116. What was the occupation of Florence Nightingale?
117. In which country were the first modern Olympic Games held?
118. Who invented the light bulb?
119. How many keys are on a piano?
120. In which country was the singer Shakira born?
121. In which city does a Glaswegian live?
122. How many panels are there on a soccer ball?
123. In which game can a bullseye be scored?
124. What is the major food of the giant panda?
125. In which continent are bees not found?
126. Where were the 2016 Olympic Games held?
127. What is the currency of the United States?
128. Who wrote the book 'Oliver Twist'?
129. What is botany the study of?
130. Triton, the largest moon in the Solar System is a moon of which planet?
131. Who sang the song 'Poker Face'?
132. Which male tennis player has won the most Grand Slam titles (as of 2019)?

133. What is the biggest island in the world?
134. How many years are there in a century?
135. Who is the present Pope (as of 2019)?
136. In which city do the Simpsons live?
137. What is the capital of Italy?
138. What two colours are linked with Halloween?
139. What colours are on the flag of Australia?
140. How many points is X worth in a game of Scrabble?
141. In which English city is Buckingham Palace?
142. In American football what position has the letters QB?
143. What is Pokémon an abbreviation of?
144. The organisation UNICEF is responsible for which group of people?
145. What does the Richter scale measure?
146. In which continent is Mount Kilimanjaro?
147. In cartoons, what bird does Sylvester the cat always chase?
148. Which Italian city is famous for its canals?
149. Which of the Australian states and territories is an island?
150. On what date do you open the first door of your advent calendar?
151. How many days are there in April?
152. On what day of the week is Mother's Day celebrated?
153. Which two oceans are joined by the Panama Canal?
154. What is the innermost colour of a rainbow?
155. Feline means relating to what sort of animal?
156. Which fruit is the most popular and most consumed in the world?
157. Which is the biggest spider in the world?
158. Where did apricots originate from?
159. Which is the smallest country in the world?
160. Who lives in a rubbish bin on 'Sesame Street'?
161. Ascorbic Acid is another name for which Vitamin-A, B or C?

162. Which singing voice is the highest pitch-Soprano, tenor or baritone?

163. Does the word 'clandestine' mean noisy, secret or colourful?

164. Which is taller-The Eiffel Tower or the Statue of Liberty?

165. In which sport might you 'spike' and 'block'-Fencing, volleyball or golf?

166. What percentage of our body weight is water? 40%, 60% or 80%?

167. A scientist who studies rocks is called a what?

168. What is the name of the outermost layer of skin?

169. Which would be most attracted to a magnet-Copper, iron or aluminium?

170. What could make Harry Potter invisible for a day?

171. What are there about 700 of in the human body, including biceps and triceps?

172. In which year was the LEGO Company founded? 1932, 1942 or 1952?

173. What is the name of the egg-hatching elephant created by Dr. Seuss?

174. What kind of animal was Willy in the movie 'Free Willy'?

175. What kind of tree do prunes come from?

176. In the film, 'Finding Nemo', what species of fish do Nemo and his father belong to?

177. What is heavier between silver or gold?

178. Which planet is known to have the greatest number of moons?

179. In the Angry Birds movie, which animals are the birds fighting against?

180. What is the collective name for a group of frogs?

181. Where does the British Prime Minister live?

182. Who is the founder of Facebook?

183. What movie franchise is famous for, "May the force be with you?"

184. Going from top left to bottom right, what is the first letter on a keyboard?
185. In which Australian city would you find the Opera House?
186. What is the name of Shrek's wife?
187. What type of food has the seeds on the outside?
188. Harry Potter plays what sport on broomsticks?
189. What is the name of molten rock before a volcanic eruption?
190. What is the name of molten rock after a volcanic eruption?
191. What continent do giraffes live in the wild?
192. Where is the Great Pyramid of Giza?
193. What is the name of female elephants?
194. In what country does the kiwi bird live?
195. Are frogs cold-blooded or warm blooded?
196. What is the top colour in a rainbow?
197. What is the name of the biggest country near New Zealand?
198. What colour are Smurfs?
199. What country's national flag has a maple leaf in the middle?
200. How many bones do sharks have?
201. What is the name of Microsoft's gaming console?
202. What is the name for a female fox?
203. What is the square root of 81?
204. What month is between August and October?
205. How many seconds are there in a minute and a half?
206. What type of Christmas decoration consists of thin strips of sparkling material on a long thread?
207. How many syllables are there in the word encyclopaedia?
208. How many members were in the group the Beatles?
209. What galaxy is Earth located in?
210. What sport is played at Wimbledon?
211. What is the name of a person who studies weather?
212. What is Harry Potter's middle name?
213. What colour is the M in the McDonald's symbol?

214. How often are the Commonwealth Games held?

215. In Thomas the Tank Engine, what colour is Percy?

216. Who does Paddington Bear come to live with?

217. How many players in a field hockey team?

218. What shape is a STOP sign?

219. What colours are on the flag of Japan?

220. What is the 11th letter of the English alphabet?

221. What colour bandana does Raphael wear in the Teenage Mutant Ninja Turtles?

222. Who were Peter Rabbit's three sisters?

223. What is a baby goat called?

224. Who is Batman's crime fighting partner?

225. What is the distance around a circle called?

226. What is a third of 150?

227. In the nursery rhyme, who sat on the wall and had a great fall?

228. What animal became Shrek's offsider/best friend?

229. In 'Charlie & The Chocolate Factory', who kept chewing on the gum?

230. What Australian actor starred in the movie, 'The Greatest Showman'?

231. How many times of its own weight can an ant pull?

232. Our body contains gold. Which body part has the most gold in it?

233. Which animal runs faster than a horse, and can live longer than a camel without water?

234. Which bird's nostrils are at the end of its beak?

235. What is dry ice chemically known as?

236. A snow flake has how many sides?

237. Which dog can run the fastest?

238. How many eyes does an earthworm have?

239. How much does one litre of water weigh?

240. What is Aurora Borealis more commonly known as?

241. What is the most common non-contagious disease in the world?

242. Which is the smallest ocean in the world?

243. In which sport can you get into a headlock?

244. Which soft, green egg shaped fruit comes from New Zealand?

245. How many points are scored for a touchdown in American football?

246. Who does Alice follow to a hole into Wonderland?

247. How many points does a team get for a win in a football (soccer) match?

248. What is the first letter in the Greek alphabet?

249. How many milligrams make up one gram?

250. What is the name of Harry Potter's pet owl?

251. What is the capital of Hawaii?

252. What form of travel does a witch favour?

253. Saint Patrick is the Patron saint of which country?

254. In sport, what is an MVP?

255. On a keyboard, what letter is between B and M?

256. In Australian football, how many points are awarded for a goal?

257. In the TV series Friends, which two characters were brother and sister?

258. How many terms can a person serve as President of the United States?

259. What was the first name of the composer Mozart?

260. What is one quarter as a percentage?

261. What is the capital city of Spain?

262. How many minutes are there in four hours?

263. How many horns did a triceratops have?

264. Who wrote the book 'A Christmas Carol'?

265. If an agreement is verbal, is it written or spoken?

266. In what country would you find the cities of Edinburgh and Glasgow?

267. What name is given to the line drawn from the centre of a circle to its edge?

268. Which is the only vowel to appear in every day of the week?

269. How many languages does a bilingual person speak?

270. In the animal kingdom, a mallard is a species of what?

271. Beginning with V, what name is given to an animal with a backbone?

272. How many millimetres in eight centimetres?

273. Which American sportswear brand is known by the letters NB?

274. In which American state is Hollywood?

275. In computers, the Apple Mac is short for what word?

276. Patience is a card game for how many players?

277. Jamie-Lynn Spears is the younger sister of which American singer?

278. Which author wrote the 'Chronicles of Narnia' series of books?

279. Bludgers and Quaffles are used in which wizarding sport?

280. How often is the Rugby World Cup played?

281. Who created the animated series 'The Simpsons'?

282. Online shopping store Amazon was founded in which year-1994, 1995 or 1996?

283. What does Ralph break in the sequel to 'Wreck it Ralph'?

284. What is the first consonant in the English alphabet?

285. How many Kings are in a standard pack of playing cards?

286. How many syllables in the word octopus?

287. Beginning with O, which gas is essential for us to breathe?

288. In what month of 2018 did Prince Harry marry Meaghan Markle?

289. Beginning with O, which layer protects the Earth from harmful rays?

290. What name is commonly given to a pizza with toppings of ham and pineapple?

291. What colour falls between yellow and blue on a rainbow?
292. A gosling is the young of which animal?
293. In 'Hickory Dickory Dock', what time did the clock strike?
294. In which Disney movie would you hear the song 'Hakuna Matata'?
295. Which film released in 2018 was based on life in Wakanda?
296. Lima is the capital city of which South American country?
297. What are the bits of paper thrown at a bride and groom at a wedding ceremony?
298. On what part of a scorpion would you find its sting?
299. Which actor played the part of Mr Bean?
300. With which sport do you associate the Davis Cup?
301. Who is the President of Russia (as of 2019)?
302. What is the name for a young swan?
303. What is the widest river in the world?
304. What is the name of Greg's younger brother in the 'Diary of a Wimpy Kid' books?
305. Grandfather, cuckoo and alarm are all types of what?
306. How many hours in four days?
307. Which code is made up of dots and dashes?
308. How many signs of the Chinese zodiac are there?
309. On what continent would you find Victoria Falls?
310. In which American city would you find the Bears, the Cubs and the White Sox?
311. How many metres in length is an Olympic sized swimming pool?
312. Hans Christian Anderson wrote the book 'The Ugly' what?
313. What colour are the benches of the House of Representatives in Australia's Parliament House?
314. In which country is the city Johannesburg?
315. What is another name for a four sided shape?
316. Is oil lighter or heavier than water?
317. 3, 6, 12, 24… what number is next?

318. The Statue of Liberty was gifted to the United States by which country?
319. Where did the game of badminton originate?
320. What vegetable is green and looks like a tree?
321. What is the name of the toy cowboy in 'Toy Story'?
322. Which fictional detective lived at 221b Baker Street?
323. What do you call a group of fish swimming together?
324. What is the fourth closest planet to the sun?
325. How many days are there in March?
326. What's the name of the fairy in 'Peter Pan'?
327. Why is Paddington Bear called Paddington?
328. What was Cinderella's coach made from?
329. What does an entomologist study?
330. What is chocolate made from?
331. In technology, what does PC stand for?
332. Where are your taste buds?
333. How many minutes in 1.5 hours?
334. Who tried to ruin Christmas in Whoville?
335. What are Maltese, Beagle and Pug?
336. What is 20% of 100?
337. Who sat on a tuffet?
338. What do vampire bats eat?
339. What colour is a raven?
340. Does an octopus give birth to live babies, or lay eggs?
341. Who wrote 'The Hobbit'?
342. What is a mammal with a pouch for its young called?
343. What is the name for the imaginary line around the centre of the Earth?
344. Where in your body is your larynx?
345. Which types of dogs pull sleds?
346. What is the shortest month of the year?
347. Is a boa a lizard or a snake?
348. What do you call the middle part of an atom?
349. Which rodent has no tail?
350. What butter made from?

351. How many eyes does a horseshoe crab have?
352. Which gas is found in soda water?
353. What is the national sport of China?
354. What is the next number in the following sequence– 7, 14, 21, 28?
355. Is the temperature of the moon higher or lower during the day?
356. Your blood type is determined by the genes you inherit from your parents: True or False?
357. What is three-fifths of 50?
358. Convection, Frontal and Relief are the three main types of clouds, rainfall, or winds?
359. An ostrich's eye is bigger than its brain. True or false?
360. Which ocean separates Africa and Australia?
361. Is a pumpkin a fruit or a vegetable?
362. Which came first-the slinky or Lego?
363. Where was the fortune cookie actually invented?
364. Where does SpongeBob work?
365. In the 'Thomas the Tank Engine' series, who is the head of the railway?
366. What is Peppa Pig's little brother called?
367. The clock and bell Big Ben is in which city?
368. In which game does the referee show a red card if a player knowingly hurts another player?
369. How many players are in a cricket team?
370. What ocean is the American state of California next to?
371. The Mounties are policemen in which country?
372. What number do you dial for emergency services in Australia?
373. Which tree shares its name with a part of the hand?
374. On which part of the body would you wear a mitten?
375. Which organs in the body allow you to take air in and breathe it out again?
376. In which country is the supposed to be a sea monster called the Loch Ness Monster?

377. What is sometimes dressed in clothes and put into a field to scare off birds?

378. What inflatable pretend building is popular for children to jump and play on?

379. Mayfair is the most expensive property on which board game?

380. New Year's Day is in which month?

381. What does D.I.Y. stand for?

382. What is the name of the building you visit to borrow books?

383. In legend, who lived in a castle called Camelot?

384. What colour are taxi cabs in New York?

385. What did the three bears have for breakfast before Goldilocks ate it?

386. A bicep is a muscle in which part of the body?

387. How many leaves does a lucky clover normally have?

388. In Victorian times what was a penny farthing?

389. Starting with the letter 'D', what do you often see and imagine when sleeping?

390. A baguette is what type of food?

391. Which famous waterfall can be found on the USA-Canada border?

392. Which language is the most spoken in the world: English, Spanish, or Mandarin Chinese?

393. In which continent is Morocco?

394. Which large country is to the south of the USA?

395. Freddie Mercury was leader singer with which legendary poop group?

396. Is Beethoven famous for pop music, classical music, or jazz?

397. A caddy is the person who carries a player's bag in which sport?

398. Which American boxer was known as 'The Greatest'?

399. The ukulele looks like a small version of which instrument?

400. In which athletics event is a long stick used to jump over a high bar?
401. What do camels store in their humps: water, fat, or milk?
402. What does a caterpillar eventually turn into?
403. What colour is the gemstone rugby?
404. True or false-Mercury is often used in thermometers?
405. Does the air we breathe contain mostly oxygen, nitrogen or carbon dioxide?
406. In computing what does the abbreviation WWW stand for?
407. What is the hardest known natural material?
408. Who owns the chocolate factory in the book 'Charlie and the Chocolate Factory'?
409. Which fictional reindeer has a glowing red nose?
410. Which religious leader lives in the Vatican?
411. Which flower is used on Remembrance Day?
412. Haggis is a traditional food in which country?
413. What type of animal is an emu?
414. What colour are the flowers of the buttercup?
415. Which gas is balloon gas, which is used to fill party balloons that float in the air?
416. Where is the largest pyramid in the world-Egypt, Peru or Mexico?
417. In what year did women first get the vote in the United Kingdom-1906, 1918 or 1923?
418. What is a ten sided shape called?
419. What is the name of a German breed of dog with a long body and short legs?
420. What is 56 divided by 4?
421. How many books are there in the Harry Potter series?
422. What is a young dolphin called?
423. In what continent are the Andes Mountains?
424. In which European country is the world's tallest bridge?
425. Finish this saying- i before e, except after.....?
426. What is the currency used in Australia?

427. A toucan is a type of what?
428. What instrument is used to measure angles in geometry?
429. Which day of the week is the Muslim Holy Day?
430. In which board game do you draw the meaning of a word?
431. What is the largest cat in the world?
432. What bird is the symbol of peace?
433. The word 'Ketchup' comes from which language?
434. What would you do with a futon?
435. Which nursery-rhyme character mislaid a flock of sheep?
436. Which of the following will not dissolve in water, salt, sugar or sand?
437. What is the name for the coloured part of the eye?
438. What is 2,845 to the nearest 1000?
439. In terms of the Internet, what is media-sharing?
440. What is the area of a right angle triangle with width 12cm and length 6cm?
441. What is the mean of this data: 11, 14, 17, 18, 20?
442. What do the numbers around a swimming pool tell you?
443. What is the name of the person who conducts an orchestra?
444. What is the difference between 6.3 and 2.4?
445. Which word describes the moment a seed begins to grow?
446. What is the product of 3 and 6?
447. The oboe is part of which instrumental family?
448. The prefix "Un" (as in "Unhappy") means what?
449. Which string instrument is often rested on the chin?
450. The program which you use to access the internet is called what?
451. How many months are there in a leap year?
452. What is an invertebrate?
453. Which musical instrument is played by Bart Simpson's sister?
454. What does "WiFi" stand for?

455. What is 33 to the nearest 10?
456. What is the source of power in an electrical circuit?
457. In 'The Muppets' what was Kermit?
458. In the initials FIFA, what does the first F stand for?
459. The Micra was made by which car company?
460. What is used by a builder to check something is level?
461. What is a baby whale called?
462. What name is given to the Japanese craft of paper folding?
463. According to the nursery rhyme when is the day that the teddy bears have their picnic?
464. What colour is sepia?
465. What are the metal hoops that you place your feet in when horse riding?
466. In volleyball what do players hit the ball with?
467. A strudel is usually filled with which fruit?
468. Claustrophobia is the fear of what?
469. What name is given to a yacht with two hulls?
470. Which two of the human's major senses begin with 'T'?
471. What does the 'I' stand for in IT?
472. Which continent is a Zebra's natural habitat?
473. What is the study of handwriting called?
474. Where is the thickest skin on your body?
475. What is the name of the dress worn by a ballerina?
476. What gas propels the cork from a champagne bottle?
477. What facial feature is missing from the painting 'Mona Lisa'?
478. Which triangle are ships and planes said to disappear in?
479. How many walls surround a squash court?
480. Which number does not exist in Roman Numerals?
481. How many points is a yellow ball worth in snooker?
482. What kind of animals were Cupid, Donner and Blitzen?
483. What shape is a sumo wrestling ring?
484. What is a new-born deer called?
485. Does a millipede have more, less or exactly 1,000 feet?

486. Which is largest - cello, viola or double bass?

487. How many members make up a water polo team?

488. What is a male sheep called?

489. Along with white, what two other colours appear on the Italian flag?

490. Which stimulant is found in tea and coffee?

491. How many spaces are in a noughts-and-crosses frame?

492. How many red balls are there at the start of a snooker game?

493. What name is given to a baby kangaroo?

494. What is the most times a day of the week can occur in two months?

495. What was the first animal in space?

496. Which units are used to measure sound intensity?

497. What colour is the skin of a kiwi fruit?

498. How many pockets does a snooker table have?

499. What do your arteries carry from your heart?

500. What is the plural of woman?

501. What is the musical term for the words which make up a song?

502. What is the plural of ox?

503. What is the number 7 worth in 6.7?

504. How do you move with the ball in basketball?

505. In tennis, when you hit the ball before it touches the ground, it is called a what?

506. How many faces does a dodecahedron have?

507. What is the number 8 worth in 4.089?

508. What is the only stringed instrument in an orchestra which isn't played with a bow?

509. What do we call the bottom number of a fraction?

510. Which percussion instrument has keys?

511. What time on an analogue clock is 19:40?

512. When playing netball which foot is not allowed to move when you have the ball?

513. What is espresso?

514. In ice hockey what shape is a puck?
515. What do snakes use to listen with?
516. Which is the saltiest of the main oceans?
517. How many E's are there in the word Experience?
518. What type of creature is a Black Widow?
519. What does a koala have for its main source of food?
520. Which word beginning with "S" is the name given to a group of bees?
521. Which bird is the symbol of the USA?
522. How many times does the letter 'S' appear in Mississippi?
523. What type of triangle has equal sides and angles?
524. What is a man-made lake in which water is stored called?
525. Which part of a tree is cork made from?
526. What are the corners of a shape also known as?
527. How many sets of teeth do most mammals have?
528. Which planet in our solar system has the fewest letters in its name?
529. What is a small segment of garlic called?
530. Complete the band name with a fruit... Red Hot _____?
531. What word can go after "roller" and before "board"
532. What type of creature is a stingray?
533. How does 4.20pm appear on a 24-hour clock?
534. If something turns in the opposite direction to the hands of a clock, what is it called?
535. Which way does vertical go?
536. How long does it take the Earth to rotate once on its axis?
537. How many pairs of ribs does a human have?
538. What is a third of 1200?
539. Winnie the Pooh lived in which wood?
540. In song, how many times is Happy Birthday referred to before naming the person?
541. What colour is Noddy's hat?
542. Tsunami is another name for what type of wave?
543. What is a baby rabbit called?

544. In which country is the city of Vancouver?
545. In which month is American Thanksgiving?
546. What food do most sharks live on?
547. The person who draws or paints the pictures found in a book is called the what?
548. What is three quarters of 1 metre in centimetres?
549. Which major compass point is on the right?
550. Where would you write the address on a postcard?
551. How many syllables are in the word 'microorganism'?
552. What types of harmful gases surround the Earth?
553. When we have very little rain causing a water shortage, what is this called?
554. What is the name of the place where rocks are extracted from the ground?
555. What number is represented by the Roman numeral D?
556. Where is the rattle in a rattlesnake?
557. What name is given to small cubes of fried bread served with soup?
558. Alphabetically, which is the first of the days of the week?
559. Would you eat, play or sit on a sitar?
560. How many syllables are in the word 'friendliness'?
561. Which feature lets you jump between web pages online?
562. Is copper magnetic?
563. What is the collective noun for geese?
564. Grapefruits, oranges, lemons and limes are high in which vitamin?
565. Who are Bart Simpson's parents?
566. What was developed to experience the excitement of surfing on land?
567. What colour are dalmatians when they are born?
568. The Tropic of Capricorn cuts what continent into two fairly equal halves?
569. Whose official plane is Air Force One?
570. What type of drink is Earl Grey?

571. How many pawns are on a chessboard at the start of a game of chess?
572. What collective name is given to the structure of bones in the body?
573. What is the name of Garfield's canine friend?
574. In Scrabble, how many points is the letter O worth?
575. Which animal is featured on the logo of the car manufacturer Porsche?
576. What type of pie is typically left out for Santa on Christmas Eve?
577. According to April Fool's Day tradition, what time should all pranks cease?
578. What is the boy in the DreamWorks logo holding in his hand?
579. Which of the Seven Dwarfs had the longest name?
580. How many years of marriage are celebrated on a golden anniversary?
581. Which two colours are most frequently confused in colour blindness?
582. How many teeth do human adults have?
583. What is the young of a shark called?
584. How many syllables are in the word 'Capacity'?
585. What is twice the amount of 345?
586. People illegally viewing or changing computer systems are known as what?
587. What is 7,891 rounded to the nearest 1,000?
588. Which breed of dog is commonly raced?
589. What colour is Scooby Doo's collar in the cartoons?
590. Which superhero wears an iron suit?
591. In which century do we live?
592. Which Disney movie includes a flying house and a bird named Kevin?
593. What are the sides of the river called?
594. What is the plural of deer, the animal?
595. Which continent has the fewest flowering plants?

596. How many 5's are there in 45?
597. TRUE or FALSE - Bones do not grow
598. Which shape has only one edge?
599. Which shape has a square face and four triangular faces?
600. What are the little yellow people in 'Despicable Me' called?
601. What is 156cm to the nearest metre?
602. What is the name of Hermione Granger's pet cat in Harry Potter?
603. In 'Snow White' what does the Prince do to wake her up?
604. If a clock hand moves from 12 to 1 how many degrees has it turned?
605. In order to grow, what does a snake need to shed?
606. What is the title of the fourth Harry Potter film?
607. The skin of a snake is covered with what?
608. Fiji is in which ocean?
609. How many horns is a unicorn supposed to have?
610. What sort of meat is usually in a hamburger?
611. Which flag in motor racing signals the end of the race?
612. In which part of the body are the smallest bones?
613. Which is the nearest million to 3,798,631?
614. What is a solvent?
615. What is the world's smallest, flattest and driest continent?
616. In which game is the object to gain checkmate?
617. When a material is dissolved, it makes a what?
618. How many runners are there in the 400m relay team?
619. What colour is the Great Spot on Jupiter?
620. What is the layer of air around the Earth called?
621. What colour hat is worn by Papa Smurf?
622. What does 'S' stand for in NASA?
623. What is caused by too much rain falling at once?
624. Which wireless technology allows you to transfer files from one device to another that is a short distance away?
625. What is a podcast?

626. Which character from 'Winnie the Pooh' lost his tail?
627. What are a pig's feet called?
628. The precious stone, a pearl, can be found in what?
629. Which came first, zips, velcro or buttons?
630. How many coins are in Australia's currency?
631. What name is given to a fox's tail?
632. 'Supercalifragilisticexpialidocious' comes from which Disney movie?
633. How many edges are there around an Australian 50 cent coin?
634. Alphabetically, which is the second of the 12 calendar months?
635. Who had a hit with Firework?
636. Is a jellyfish a mineral, vegetable or animal?
637. What shape is the target in archery?
638. Which direction do you go if you are abseiling?
639. In printing, uppercase are what type of letters?
640. Alphabetically, what is the first sign of the zodiac?
641. What name is given to the calm area in the centre of a hurricane?
642. What is the power produced by the sun called?
643. Name the seventh planet from the sun?
644. What sport does Adam Scott play?
645. How many valves does a trumpet have?
646. The Himalaya Mountains are in which continent?
647. Full moons occur approximately how often?
648. What type of animal is a kingfisher?
649. What is the natural home for rabbits?
650. What colours are on the flag of China?
651. What was Captain Cook's first name?
652. Where would you see a ringmaster?
653. Polar bears live closer to the North or South Pole?
654. What does a barometer measure?
655. Every insect has a head, thorax and a what?
656. How many quarters in 3 wholes?

657. Which has the biggest population-China, Japan or India?
658. How many millimetres in two-and-a-half centimetres?
659. Which board game has pieces called King, Queen and Bishop?
660. If you divide 60 by 11 what is the remainder?
661. By how many hours Australian Eastern Standard Time is ahead of Australian Western Standard Time?
662. Who played the part of Harry Potter in the films?
663. How many holes are there in a full round of golf?
664. Which river flows through London?
665. What is the name of Han Solo's ship?
666. The Vikings came from Scandinavia-True or false?
667. In the original Jacksons line up how many were there?
668. The Knicks would take on the Nets in which sport?
669. Rap singing originated in what country?
670. In American baseball, where do the Braves come from?
671. True or false? Scarlet is a bright red colour.
672. Which atmospheric gas is the most common?
673. The design stamped on each side of an Oreo cookie has how many flowers?
674. What is the name of Garfield the cat's owner?
675. How many countries share a border with Germany-3, 6 or 9?
676. Who was the host of the Muppet Show?
677. In Google's logo, what colour is the capital G?
678. What is the name of Homer Simpson's father?
679. What colour is Mr Nosey in the Mr Men books?
680. How many zeros are there in the number 10 million?
681. Approximately how many teaspoons of sugar are there in a 330ml can of regular Cola-3, 5 or 7?
682. In which hand is the Statue of Liberty's torch?
683. Do books have even numbered pages on the right or left hand side?
684. How many sides are there on a standard pencil?
685. Does a merry-go-round turn clockwise or anticlockwise?

686. What is the unit of measurement used to measure the height of horse?
687. How many pedals do most modern pianos have?
688. In nautical terms, what is the opposite of port on a ship?
689. What is one quarter of 1,000?
690. Which Tasmanian marsupial is known for its fiery temper?
691. What is the Roman numeral IX in Arabic numeral form?
692. Which animal is known as the 'Ship of the Desert'?
693. What colour symbolises peace?
694. What letter is between T and U on a standard keyboard?
695. Which team won the AFL Premiership in 2018?
696. What colour train was Edward in the 'Thomas the Tank Engine' stories?
697. A hippo has six toes on each foot-True or false?
698. What word is used for an extremely tall building?
699. Which of these words is NOT an adverb-slowly, lovely or quietly?
700. What is at the centre of our solar system?
701. How long can a player hold a ball in netball?
702. What was a boomerang first used for-a weapon, a toy or an ornament?
703. Who was the hero rat in the animated film 'Ratatouille'?
704. In which sport can you 'hang ten'?
705. Peter Parker is Spiderman-True or false?
706. Which part of your body contains a hammer and an anvil?
707. Which of these shapes is NOT four sided-trapezium, parallelogram or hexagon?
708. What colour tennis clothes were players once required to wear?
709. What mineral can harm Superman?
710. What position does Cho Chang play on Ravenclaw's Quidditch team-beater, chaser or seeker?
711. Which of these wears the heaviest equipment in sport-baseball catcher, ice hockey goalie or cricketer?

712. How many millimetres in a kilometre?
713. What German car logo has four rings linked together?
714. What is Bugs Bunny's three-word catchphrase?
715. In what country is Uluru?
716. Los Angeles is the capital city of California-True or false?
717. What is the name of Horrid Henry's well-behaved younger brother?
718. On which continent did the potato plant originate?
719. How many feet does a ballet dancer use for a pirouette?
720. What is Rugrat Tommy's surname?
721. In which continent is Canada?
722. Dorothy the Dinosaur is friends with which band?
723. What is the witch's house made of in 'Hansel and Gretel'?
724. On which continent is the Cape of Good Hope?
725. Who was Buzz Lightyear's enemy in 'Toy Story'?
726. How many thieves was Ali Baba associated with?
727. In which country are the cities of Mumbai and Delhi?
728. What kind of word can be a person, place or thing?
729. What three colours make up the flag of France?
730. Who does Timothy Q Mouse help with his problems?
731. How many books are in the 'Chronicles of Narnia' series-3, 5 or 7?
732. What point on a compass is between north and north east?
733. Which country has an area called the Yukon Territory?
734. 'Mamma Mia' is a musical/film based on the songs of which band?
735. White cats are often deaf-True or false?
736. How many holes in a ten-pin bowling ball?
737. In which continent is the Amazon River?
738. Badminton is an Olympic sport-True or false?
739. Which Hogwarts house has a badger on its crest?
740. Whose 'eyes are orange', 'tongue is black' and who 'has purple prickles all over his back'?
741. What is it called when a bear goes to sleep all winter?
742. What material is normally used to make pottery?

743.   Will you float better in salt or fresh water?
744.   The Wimbledon Tennis tournament is played on what type of surface?
745.   Alpha, beta and gamma are the first three letters of which alphabet?
746.   In what book is Wilbur the pig saved from the slaughterhouse by a spider?
747.   Which planet in the solar system has the largest canyon-Venus, Earth or Mars?
748.   The Pope is the leader of which faith?
749.   Reduce, reuse and what is the third R?
750.   What is the colour of the official ball used in a water polo match?
751.   What does the Internet and text abbreviation IMHO stand for?
752.   Which little piggy had roast beef-first, second or third one?
753.   Which of these is biggest-35 per cent, two fifths or three tenths?
754.   Which of these is not one of the colours on a Rubik's Cube-white, purple or orange?
755.   What kind of sandwiches does SpongeBob like to eat?
756.   How many points do you get for an unconverted try in rugby union?
757.   You can sneeze with your eyes open-True or false?
758.   Who was the pirate in 'Peter Pan'?
759.   What season is it in Australia when its summer in the UK?
760.   In the series 'Ben 10', what is Ben's real surname?
761.   How many stars on the flag of New Zealand?
762.   In which Caribbean country was Rhianna born-Jamaica, Haiti or Barbados?
763.   How many oceans are there on Earth?
764.   What is the national language of Mexico?
765.   How did flesh eating dinosaurs walk-on their hind legs, all fours or tip-toes?

766. At what temperature does water boil?

767. In which continent is Timbuktu?

768. Which was discovered first-Uranus or Neptune?

769. What is a synonym?

770. How long does it take for light from the Sun to reach Earth-8, 18 or 80 minutes?

771. In which city does the final stage of the World Grand Prix racing event take place in 'Cars 2'?

772. What country is singer Shakira from-USA, Cuba or Colombia?

773. What word best describes the weather in Siberia?

774. What is the verb that means to post a message on Twitter?

775. Who does legend say stole from the rich and gave to the poor?

776. Which of these did the caterpillar not eat in 'The Very Hungry Caterpillar'-bananas, pears or oranges?

777. In netball, which two players are allowed to score goals?

778. Peking duck is associated with which country?

779. Which plane has right of way at an airport-a plane landing or taking off?

780. What colour was Tinky Winky in 'Teletubbies'?

781. What do the Chinese name their years after?

782. What is the hand signal for 'paper in 'Rock, Paper, Scissors'?

783. In which ocean is Sri Lanka?

784. What is the word for a lens that curves outward in the centre-convex or concave?

785. What did the Ancient Greeks use for soap-clay, olive oil or butter?

786. Approximately how long is the index finger of the Statue of Liberty-1m, 2.5m or 6m?

787. What colour is the edible flesh of a pomegranate fruit?

788. How many pieces are there in a domino set?

789. Super Mario is a plumber-True or false?

790. What part of your body are canines?
791. What was the name of the crab in 'The Little Mermaid'?
792. How are Manx cats different from most other cats?
793. How long does a Premier League football match usually last?
794. How many of the Seven Dwarfs names end in 'y'?
795. How many points do you get for hitting a bullseye in archery-5, 10 or 15?
796. Which television series has had annual 'Treehouse of Horror' Halloween specials?
797. How many months of the year have the letter 'B' in their name?
798. What is the top number in a fraction called?
799. On a child's birthday in Denmark, it is traditional to fly what out of a window-a kite, a balloon or a flag?
800. How many children were there in 'The Sound of Music'?
801. What kind of tree does a kookaburra sit in in the famous song?
802. What is the name of the oven in which ceramic pots are fired?
803. Who was the strongman of Roman mythology-Hercules, Hermes or Hades?
804. In which continent is the country Kenya?
805. What was the name of Nemo's mother in 'Finding Nemo'?
806. A stealth plane is invisible to radar-True or false?
807. Which country is further south in Europe-Italy or Spain?
808. Which mountain range is Mt Everest in?
809. What is a book of maps and charts called?
810. What is the dish calamari made from?
811. Do gliders have a motor?
812. What are deltoids, trapezius and quadriceps-muscles, bones or viruses?
813. What does a philatelist collect?
814. What is the most common number of people on a jury?

815. Which covers a larger area-a hurricane or tornado?

816. Twenty20 is a short form of which popular sport?

817. How many basic leg positions are there in ballet?

818. What sort of creature was Scrat in the 'Ice Age' movies?

819. How many lines does a limerick poem have?

820. Iceland contains about 200 volcanoes-True or false?

821. Which American singer sang 'Born This Way' and 'Poker Face'?

822. What is the natural force that powers sailing boats?

823. In netball, what position does GD stand for?

824. By what name are the Arctic's Inuit people commonly known?

825. What is a caravel-ship, gun or bridge?

826. What is an optometrist concerned with-ears, eyes or nose?

827. Gargamel is the enemy of which pint-sized blue characters?

828. What vitamin are oranges and other citrus fruits a good source of?

829. What colour card is shown to a football (soccer) player to indicate he/she is out of the game?

830. The Great Fire of London started in a butcher's shop-True or false?

831. What small triangular piece of glass can create rainbows by bending light?

832. What colour road do you follow to reach Oz's Emerald City?

833. What awoke Sleeping Beauty from her deep sleep?

834. What shape is the name for a baseball field?

835. Origami is a paper craft that comes from which country?

836. What is coffee made from?

837. What does a C represent in Roman Numerals?

838. On which side of your body is your appendix?

839. Which American city is the world headquarters of the United Nations?

840. What is the time machine called that Doctor Who travels in?

841. Who fell into the chocolate river in the book 'Charlie and the Chocolate Factory'?

842. What country is the band U2 from-Sweden, England or Ireland?

843. What is the main crop of China?

844. In what sport would you perform a 'slam dunk'?

845. What was the name of the princess in the Disney film 'Aladdin'?

846. What is the name of the swing used by acrobats in a circus?

847. What direction lies directly opposite south-east on a compass?

848. Who is the teenage boy Anthony Horowitz writes about?

849. Where is the Sea of Tranquillity?

850. What sport is Babe Ruth famous for playing?

851. Where is the film 'How to Train Your Dragon' set?

852. What shape is a symphony orchestra arranged in-circle, semi-circle or square?

853. What breed of dog is most often used by the world's police forces?

854. What name does SpongeBob's pet snail answer to?

855. Former US President Ronald Reagan used to be an actor-True or false?

856. What does Goldilocks eat in the Three Bear's home?

857. How does a referee start a football (soccer) game?

858. What is Hannah Montana's name when she is a normal schoolgirl?

859. Which coast of Australia did Captain Cook reach first?

860. An emu cannot walk backwards-True or false?

861. What job does Pingu's father do?

862. A tangelo is a hybrid fruit of a tangerine and what other fruit?

863. What do we call the fields where rice is grown?

864. What red flower is worn as a symbol of remembrance?
865. Which fish could be a bull, hammerhead or tiger?
866. What metal are Olympic gold medals actually made of?
867. Which is the last of Disney's Seven Dwarfs alphabetically?
868. What is the name of the Chinese art of using needles to block pain and cure illness?
869. What is the shape of the course that a horse race takes place on?
870. Mongolia shares a border with Russia-True or false?
871. What is the name of the main character in 'Diary of a Wimpy Kid'?
872. What sport uses stones and small brooms?
873. What ocean separates Europe from the United States?
874. What artificial body of water surrounds a castle?
875. Who does Wile E Coyote chase but never catches?
876. Which of these countries is an island nation-Spain, Turkey or Japan?
877. 'Tomorrow When the War Began' is a film set in which country?
878. What are carp, herring and salmon types of?
879. The Davis Cup is an event in which sport?
880. What form of transport was called a horseless carriage when first invented?
881. Which US city is known for its casinos, hotels and bright lights?
882. Which cartoon character has the catchphrase 'Be vewy, vewy quiet; I'm hunting wabbits'?
883. What types of events were held at the Circus Maximus in Ancient Rome?
884. Elvis Presley sang about what colour suede shoes?
885. Which teeth are used for grinding up food-incisors, canines or molars?
886. Which continent almost doubles in winter?
887. What is the only species of cat that will live and hunt in a group?

888. What are Caribbean steel drums traditionally made out of-old cars, oil drums or tyre rims?
889. What word is a cross between smoke and fog?
890. What score is a perfect game in ten-pin bowling?
891. In which ocean is the Mariana Trench-the deepest point on the earth's surface?
892. What is the name of a play in which all words are sung instead of spoken?
893. What sea creature has eyes the size of a volleyball?
894. What is bratwurst?
895. What fruit is dried to make raisins?
896. Zebras are native to which continent?
897. How many teeth does Bruce the shark have in 'Finding Nemo'-102, 202 or 302?
898. Chocolate was once used as medicine-True or false?
899. Who was the first ever boys' action figure-Action Man, Superman or GI Joe?
900. How many degrees is a circle divided into?
901. What is the last word in the Adele song 'Someone like____'?
902. What results when the Moon gets between the Earth and the Sun?
903. What country used to known as Persia-Iran, Greece or Egypt?
904. Chimpanzees can catch chickenpox-True or false?
905. What colour is the video game character Sonic the Hedgehog?
906. Which is the deepest canal in the world?
907. Which three European countries have a road system called the Autobahn?
908. Which city hosts the Australian Grand Prix?
909. Which city is known as the 'Big Apple'?
910. Bats are members of the bird family-True or false?
911. Which swashbuckling pirate was played by Johnny Depp?

912. What is the name of a mythical, one horned, horse-like creature?

913. What colour was the original Nintendo Wi games console?

914. Which musical instrument accompanies a flamenco dancer?

915. What is both a name for a tornado and a game played on the floor?

916. Which is further north-Sydney Opera House or Big Ben?

917. What swordsman leaves the mark of a 'Z'?

918. What gas can be put in tubes to make colourful, bright lights?

919. How many days are in 72 hours?

920. On average, watching TV for an hour burns more calories than sleeping for an hour-True or false?

921. What colour is the submarine from the Beatles song?

922. The first set of traffic lights were installed in 1868-True or false?

923. Who wrote the book 'James and the Giant Peach'?

924. In the movie 'Up', Charles Muntz's dogs have what unusual talent?

925. What items are used to send messages in Semaphore Code?

926. Who tries to get his friend to eat green eggs and ham?

927. What do chickens, turtles and spiders all have in common?

928. What's the board part of a skateboard called-plank, deck or block?

929. Children in Ancient Rome played board games-True or false

930. How long did Phileas Fogg take to go around the world?

931. What colour was only worn by the families of the emperor or senators in Ancient Rome-yellow, white or purple?

932. Cartoon stars Daffy and Donald are both which type of animal?

933. What language was spoken in Ancient Rome?
934. What type of electricity makes hair stick to a comb or tumble-dried clothes make a crackling sound?
935. Which of these games was once a real Olympic event-dodge ball, tug-of-war or hopscotch?
936. The silver fern is the symbol for which national rugby union team?
937. What is haiku?
938. How many teeth does an elephant have?
939. What type of dance has the same name as a sauce?
940. Where did Robin Hood live?
941. According to legend, what was the name of King Arthur's wizard friend?
942. Which of these musical instruments is known as 'curly horn'-trombone, trumpet or bugle?
943. Which clouds are the highest-stratus, cumulus or cirrus?
944. In which sport would you face a doosra, flipper or bouncer?
945. What did the Ugly Duckling grow up to be?
946. What was red about the Red Baron, the WW1 flying ace?
947. What fictional metal are Wolverine's claws made from in 'X-Men'?
948. What instrument does a scientist use to look at very small objects?
949. What story features Tiny Tim and Ebenezer Scrooge?
950. What does an entomologist study-fish, rocks or insects?
951. What creatures took over the ship in 'Madagascar'?
952. What character fell asleep for 20 years after a bowling match?
953. Who taught Dr Dolittle to talk to the animals?
954. Who lives in the second-floor girls' bathroom at Hogwarts?
955. What kind of an animal is mustang?
956. What shape was the table used by King Arthur in Camelot?

957. Who is Woody and Buzz Lightyear's owner in 'Toy Story'?
958. Water boils at 32°F-True or false?
959. Is a city a rural or urban area?
960. How many polo ponies are on a field at one time-8, 10 or 12?
961. Times Square is a famous district in which US city?
962. Which Doctor Who villains come from the planet Mondas?
963. What is Michelangelo's David-a sculpture, a painting, a poem?
964. Will the pupil of your eye get bigger or smaller in a dark room?
965. Which of these drawing pencils is the softest-H, HB or B?
966. Which animal is the symbol for the World Wildlife Fund?
967. Where were the Ancient Olympic Games held?
968. In which country is Mount Ararat found-Spain, Turkey or France?
969. Which bear is Christopher Robin's best friend?
970. Which of these does not use a ball-snooker, ice hockey or tennis?
971. What language gave us words like stampede, avocado and bonanza?
972. May 4th is official Star Wars Day-True or false?
973. What flower is associated with the religious holiday of Easter?
974. Which band was formed in Liverpool and was known as the 'Fab Four'?
975. What kind of musical instrument is a Fender Stratocaster?
976. What do the witches in Roald Dahl's book want to turn all children into-mice, turnips or frogs?
977. Which tennis playing Williams sister has the names Ebony Starr-Venus or Serena?
978. Which of these animals is NOT nocturnal-bat, mole or guinea pig?

979. In cricket, how many runs equal a triple century?

980. What is the currency of Italy?

981. Who created the character Peter Rabbit?

982. What is a sea star more commonly known as?

983. Which golf club is used when the ball is on the green, ready to be hit into the hole?

984. October was originally what number month in the old Roman calendar?

985. In which continent is Libya?

986. What kind of creature was Manny in the 'Ice Age' films?

987. What would an Ancient Roman do with a toga-eat it, wear it or hunt with it?

988. A wedding ring is usually worn on the little finger-True or false?

989. What are you afraid of if you suffer from hydrophobia?

990. What is the main ingredient in an omelette and quiche?

991. In which continent is Hungary?

992. Shades and sunnies are two names for which fashion accessory?

993. For how many years was Nelson Mandela in prison-7, 17 or 27?

994. The word Crayola means 'oily chalk'-True or false?

995. Lisbon is the capital city of which European country?

996. Which of these is not a mountain range-Himalaya, Ganges or Rockies?

997. Which way is a TV screen size measured-horizontally or diagonally?

998. In art, acrylics and oils are types of what?

999. In horse riding which is fastest-canter, gallop or trot?

1000. Which end of the Earth is flatter-the North Pole or the South Pole?

1000 TRIVIA

QUESTIONS
FOR KIDS

The Answers

1.   The White House
2.   Blue, red, green, black, yellow
3.   R
4.   52 cards –not including 2 joker cards
5.   Football (soccer)
6.   Lighter
7.   New York City
8.   Carbon dioxide
9.   Bonjour
10.   Iron
11.   Sweden
12.   Three
13.   Carbon dioxide
14.   Four
15.   Asia
16.   Five
17.   Africa
18.   Ed Sheeran
19.   Birds
20.   Red and yellow
21.   Pinocchio
22.   True
23.   48 hours
24.   Spider
25.   England
26.   Red and white
27.   C-explorer
28.   Ostrich
29.   It freezes
30.   B-Indian
31.   Cycling
32.   True
33.   Twelve
34.   Bullseye
35.   Floors

36.   Mercury, Venus, Earth, Mars
37.   Two sets of wickets
38.   The White Witch
39.   North America
40.   Amazon Rainforest
41.   Pacific Ocean
42.   False: amphibians are vertebrate animals as they have backbones
43.   K
44.   Egypt
45.   True: it is called the femur
46.   Asia
47.   Nine
48.   Herbivores
49.   God's Plan
50.   Giraffe
51.   Paris
52.   B-7
53.   Seven
54.   South America
55.   Ariana Grande
56.   Australia
57.   Germany
58.   Barack
59.   Gryffindor
60.   G
61.   Canada
62.   Pentagon
63.   False-the left lung is smaller
64.   Neptune
65.   Pacific Ocean
66.   True
67.   A,I,O
68.   Seven
69.   Blue whale

70.   Helen Parr (Elastigirl)
71.   24
72.   Africa
73.   Six
74.   Atlantic Ocean
75.   Gotham City
76.   Robert Downey Jr
77.   Tokyo
78.   Asia
79.   Australia
80.   T
81.   Two
82.   Skull
83.   Lion
84.   V
85.   Bruno Mars
86.   False-it is below freezing
87.   B-Fish
88.   B-44, C-80, E-16
89.   True
90.   C-Giant armadillo
91.   Fish
92.   The Lego Movie
93.   Humps
94.   Africa
95.   Hermione and Ron
96.   Red and green
97.   Garlic
98.   October 31st
99.   Z
100. France
101. Digestive system
102. Nile River
103. Atlantic Ocean
104. Seven

105. O
106. Blue whale
107. A pride
108. Six
109. Oompa Loompas
110. William Shakespeare
111. H2O
112. Seven
113. Pound
114. Zn
115. Gravity
116. Nurse
117. Greece
118. Thomas Edison
119. 88
120. Colombia
121. Glasgow
122. 32
123. Darts
124. Bamboo
125. Antarctica
126. Rio de Janeiro
127. US dollar
128. Charles Dickens
129. Plants
130. Neptune
131. Lady Gaga
132. Roger Federer
133. Greenland
134. 100
135. Pope Francis
136. Springfield
137. Rome
138. Orange and black
139. Red, white, blue

140. Eight
141. London
142. Quarterback
143. Pocket Monster
144. Children
145. An earthquake
146. Africa
147. Tweety Pie
148. Venice
149. Tasmania
150. December 1st
151. 30
152. Sunday
153. Atlantic and Pacific oceans
154. Violet
155. Cat
156. Bananas
157. Tarantula
158. China
159. The Vatican
160. Oscar the Grouch
161. Vitamin C
162. Soprano
163. Secret
164. Eiffel Tower-320m Statue of Liberty-93m
165. Volleyball
166. 60%-approximately
167. Geologist
168. Epidermis
169. Iron
170. Invisibility Cloak
171. Muscles
172. 1932
173. Horton
174. Whale

175.   Plum tree
176.   Clownfish
177.   Gold
178.   Jupiter
179.   Pigs
180.   An army
181.   10 Downing Street
182.   Mark Zuckerberg
183.   Star Wars
184.   Q
185.   Sydney
186.   Fiona
187.   Strawberry
188.   Quidditch
189.   Magma
190.   Lava
191.   Africa
192.   Egypt
193.   Cows
194.   New Zealand
195.   Cold blooded
196.   Red
197.   Australia
198.   Blue
199.   Canada
200.   None
201.   X-box
202.   Vixen
203.   Nine
204.   September
205.   90 seconds
206.   Tinsel
207.   Six
208.   Four
209.   Milky Way

210. Tennis
211. A meteorologist
212. James
213. Yellow
214. Every four years
215. Green
216. The Browns
217. Eleven
218. Octagon shape
219. Red and white
220. K
221. Red
222. Flopsy, Mopsy and Cottontail
223. A kid
224. Robin
225. The circumference
226. 50
227. Humpty Dumpty
228. Donkey
229. Violet Beauregarde
230. Hugh Jackman
231. Around ten times
232. The toenails
233. Giraffe
234. Kiwi
235. Solid carbon dioxide
236. Six
237. Greyhound
238. None
239. One kilogram
240. Northern lights
241. Tooth decay
242. Arctic Ocean
243. Wrestling
244. Kiwi fruit

245. Six points
246. White rabbit
247. Three points
248. Alpha
249. 1000 milligrams
250. Hedwig
251. Honolulu
252. Broomstick
253. Ireland
254. Most Valuable Player
255. N
256. Six points
257. Ross and Monica
258. Two terms
259. Wolfgang
260. 25%
261. Madrid
262. 240 minutes
263. Three horns
264. Charles Dickens
265. Spoken
266. Scotland
267. Radius
268. A
269. Two
270. Duck
271. Vertebrate
272. 80mm
273. New Balance
274. California
275. Macintosh
276. One
277. Britney Spears
278. CS Lewis
279. Quidditch

280. Every four years
281. Matt Groening
282. 1994
283. The internet
284. B
285. Four
286. Three
287. Oxygen
288. May
289. Ozone
290. Hawaiian pizza
291. Green
292. Goose
293. One o'clock
294. The Lion King
295. Black Panther
296. Peru
297. Confetti
298. Its tail
299. Rowan Atkinson
300. Tennis
301. Vladimir Putin
302. Cygnet
303. Amazon
304. Many/Manuel
305. Clocks
306. 96 hours
307. Morse Code
308. Twelve
309. Africa
310. Chicago
311. 50 metres
312. Duckling
313. Green
314. South Africa

315. Quadrilateral
316. Lighter
317. 48
318. France
319. India
320. Broccoli
321. Woody
322. Sherlock Holmes
323. School
324. Mars
325. 31 days
326. Tinkerbell
327. He was found at Paddington Station
328. A pumpkin
329. Insects
330. Cocoa beans
331. Personal computer
332. On your tongue
333. 90 minutes
334. The Grinch
335. A breed of dog
336. Twenty
337. Little Miss Muffet
338. Blood
339. Black
340. Lays eggs
341. JRR Tolkien
342. Marsupial
343. The equator
344. In your throat
345. Huskies
346. February
347. Snake
348. Nucleus
349. Guinea pig

350. Milk
351. Ten
352. Carbon dioxide
353. Table tennis
354. 35
355. Higher
356. True
357. 30
358. Rainfall
359. True
360. Indian Ocean
361. Fruit
362. The slinky
363. San Francisco-USA
364. The Krusty Krab
365. The Fat Controller-Sir Topham Hatt
366. George Pig
367. London
368. Football-soccer
369. Eleven
370. Pacific Ocean
371. Canada
372. 000
373. Palm
374. On your hands
375. Lungs
376. Scotland
377. Scarecrow
378. Bouncy castle
379. Monopoly
380. January
381. Do It Yourself
382. Library
383. King Arthur
384. Yellow

385. Porridge
386. The arm
387. Four
388. Bicycle
389. Dream
390. Bread —long French stick of bread
391. Niagara Falls
392. Mandarin Chinese
393. Africa
394. Mexico
395. Queen
396. Classical music
397. Golf
398. Muhammad Ali
399. Guitar
400. Pole vault
401. Fat
402. Butterfly
403. Red (pink)
404. True
405. Nitrogen
406. World Wide Web
407. Diamond
408. Willy Wonka
409. Rudolph
410. The Pope
411. Poppy
412. Scotland
413. A large flightless bird
414. Yellow
415. Helium
416. Mexico
417. 1918
418. Decagon
419. Dachshund

420. Fourteen
421. Seven
422. Calf
423. South America
424. France-Millau Viaduct-height of 336.4m
425. C
426. Australian dollar
427. Bird
428. Protractor
429. Friday
430. Pictionary
431. Tiger
432. Dove
433. Chinese
434. Sleep on it
435. Little Bo Peep
436. Sand
437. Iris
438. 3000
439. Sharing music, video, photos, or other types of files over the internet
440. 36cm squared
441. 16
442. The depth of the water
443. Conductor or maestro
444. 3.9
445. Germination
446. 18
447. Woodwind
448. Not
449. Violin
450. Browser
451. 12 months
452. An animal without a spine
453. Saxophone

454. Wireless fidelity
455. 30
456. Battery
457. Frog
458. Federation
459. Nissan
460. Spirit level
461. Calf
462. Origami
463. Today
464. Brown
465. Stirrups
466. Their hands
467. Apple
468. Enclosed spaces
469. Catamaran
470. Touch, taste
471. Information
472. Africa
473. Graphology
474. Your feet
475. A tutu
476. Carbon dioxide
477. Eyebrows
478. The Bermuda Triangle
479. Four
480. Zero
481. Two points
482. Reindeer
483. Circular
484. Fawn
485. Less
486. Double bass
487. Seven
488. Ram

489. Red, green
490. Caffeine
491. Nine
492. 15
493. Joey
494. Nine
495. Dog
496. Decibels
497. Brown
498. Six
499. Blood
500. Women
501. Lyrics
502. Oxen
503. 7 tenths
504. Bouncing the ball
505. Volley
506. Twelve
507. 8 hundredths
508. Harp
509. Denominator
510. Piano
511. 20 minutes to 8-7:40pm
512. Landing foot
513. Coffee
514. Round
515. Their tongues
516. Atlantic Ocean
517. Four
518. Spider
519. Eucalyptus leaves
520. Swarm
521. Eagle
522. Four
523. Equilateral

524. Reservoir
525. Bark
526. Vertices
527. Two sets
528. Mars
529. Clove
530. Chilli Peppers
531. Skate
532. Fish
533. 16:20
534. Anticlockwise
535. Up and down
536. One day
537. Twelve
538. 400
539. Hundred Acre Wood
540. Three
541. Blue
542. Tidal wave
543. Kitten or kit
544. Canada
545. November
546. Fish
547. Illustrator
548. 75cm
549. East
550. On the right hand side
551. Six
552. Greenhouse gases
553. Drought
554. Quarry
555. D
556. In the tail
557. Croutons
558. Friday

559. Play
560. Three
561. Hyperlink
562. No
563. Gaggle
564. Vitamin C
565. Homer and Marge
566. Skateboard
567. White
568. Australia
569. US President
570. Tea
571. 16
572. Skeleton
573. Odie
574. One point
575. Horse
576. Mince pie
577. 12 noon
578. A fishing rod
579. Bashful
580. 50 years
581. Red and green
582. 32
583. Pup
584. Four
585. 690
586. Hackers
587. 8000
588. Greyhound
589. Blue
590. Iron Man
591. 21st century
592. Up
593. Banks

594. Deer
595. Antarctica
596. Nine
597. False
598. Circle
599. Pyramid
600. Minions
601. Two metres
602. Crookshanks
603. He kisses her
604. 30 degrees
605. Its skin
606. Harry Potter and the Goblet of Fire
607. Scales
608. Pacific Ocean
609. One
610. Beef
611. Chequered flag
612. Ear
613. 4 million
614. The liquid in which a material has been dissolved
615. Australia
616. Chess
617. Solution
618. Four
619. Red
620. Atmosphere
621. Red
622. Space
623. Floods
624. Bluetooth
625. A digital audio file which can be downloaded from the internet
626. Eeyore
627. Trotters

628. Oysters
629. Buttons
630. Five
631. Brush
632. Mary Poppins
633. 12 edges
634. August
635. Katy Perry
636. Animal
637. Circular
638. Downwards
639. Capital letters
640. Aquarius
641. The eye
642. Solar
643. Uranus
644. Golf
645. Three
646. Asia
647. One month/four weeks
648. Bird
649. Warrens
650. Red and yellow
651. James
652. At a circus
653. North Pole
654. Air pressure
655. Abdomen
656. Twelve quarters
657. China
658. 25mm
659. Chess
660. Five
661. Two hours
662. Daniel Radcliffe

663. 18 holes
664. Thames River
665. Millennium Falcon
666. True
667. Five
668. Basketball
669. USA
670. Atlanta
671. True
672. Nitrogen
673. Twelve
674. John
675. Nine
676. Kermit the Frog
677. Blue
678. Abraham
679. Green
680. Seven
681. About 7 teaspoons
682. Right hand
683. Left hand side
684. Six sides
685. Anticlockwise
686. Hands (1 hand =4 inches/10cm)
687. Three
688. Starboard
689. 250
690. Tasmanian Devil
691. Nine
692. Camel
693. White
694. Y
695. West Coast Eagles
696. Blue
697. False-4 toes

698. Skyscraper
699. Lovely
700. The Sun
701. Three seconds
702. As a weapon
703. Remy
704. Surfing
705. True
706. The ear
707. Hexagon
708. White
709. Kryptonite
710. Seeker
711. Ice hockey goalie
712. One million
713. Audi
714. 'What's up doc'?
715. Australia
716. False
717. Perfect Peter
718. South America
719. One foot
720. Pickles
721. North America
722. The Wiggles
723. Gingerbread
724. Africa
725. Emperor Zurg
726. 40
727. India
728. Noun
729. Red, white and blue
730. Dumbo
731. Seven
732. North-north-east

733. Canada
734. ABBA
735. True
736. Three
737. South America
738. True
739. Hufflepuff
740. Gruffalo
741. Hibernation
742. Clay
743. Salt water
744. Grass
745. Greek
746. Charlotte's Web
747. Mars
748. Roman Catholic church
749. Recycle
750. Yellow
751. In my humble/honest opinion
752. Third one
753. Two fifths
754. Purple
755. Seanut butter
756. Five points
757. False
758. Captain Hook
759. Winter
760. Tennyson
761. Four stars
762. Barbados
763. Five
764. Spanish
765. On their hind legs
766. 100°C/212°F
767. Africa

768. Uranus
769. A word that means the same as another word
770. Eight minutes
771. London
772. Colombia
773. Cold
774. Tweet
775. Robin Hood
776. Bananas
777. Goal shooter, goal attack
778. China
779. A plane landing
780. Purple
781. Animals
782. Open hand (with palms down)
783. Indian Ocean
784. Convex
785. Olive oil
786. 2.5m
787. Red
788. 28 pieces
789. True
790. Teeth
791. Sebastian
792. They have no tail
793. 90 minutes
794. Five
795. 10 points
796. The Simpsons
797. Five months
798. Numerator
799. A flag
800. Seven
801. Gum tree
802. Kiln

803. Hercules
804. Africa
805. Coral
806. True
807. Spain
808. Himalayas
809. Atlas
810. Squid
811. No
812. Muscles
813. Stamps
814. 12
815. Hurricane
816. Cricket
817. Five
818. Squirrel (sabre tooth)
819. Five
820. True
821. Lady Gaga
822. Wind
823. Goal Defence
824. Eskimos
825. Ship
826. Eyes
827. The Smurfs
828. Vitamin C
829. Red
830. False-a bakery
831. Prism
832. Yellow brick road
833. A kiss from a prince
834. Diamond
835. Japan
836. Beans
837. 100

838. Right side
839. New York City
840. The TARDIS
841. Augustus Gloop
842. Ireland
843. Rice
844. Basketball
845. Jasmine
846. Trapeze
847. North-west
848. Alex Rider
849. On the moon
850. Baseball
851. Isle of Berk
852. Semi-circle
853. German shepherd
854. Gary
855. True
856. Porridge
857. Blows a whistle
858. Miley Stewart
859. East coast
860. True
861. Postman
862. Grapefruit
863. Paddy fields
864. Poppy
865. Shark
866. Silver
867. Sneezy
868. Acupuncture
869. Oval
870. True
871. Greg (Gregory)
872. Curling

873. Atlantic Ocean
874. Moat
875. Road Runner
876. Japan
877. Australia
878. Fish
879. Tennis
880. Cars
881. Las Vegas
882. Elmer Fudd
883. Chariot races
884. Blue
885. Molars
886. Antarctica
887. Lion
888. Oil drums
889. Smog
890. 300
891. Pacific Ocean
892. Opera
893. Giant squid
894. German sausage
895. Grapes
896. Africa
897. 202
898. True
899. GI Joe
900. 360
901. You
902. Solar eclipse
903. Iran
904. True
905. Blue
906. Panama Canal
907. Germany, Austria and Switzerland

908. Melbourne
909. New York
910. False
911. Captain Jack Sparrow
912. Unicorn
913. White
914. Guitar
915. Twister
916. Big Ben
917. Zorro
918. Neon
919. Three days
920. True
921. Yellow
922. True
923. Roald Dahl
924. They can talk
925. Flags
926. Sam
927. They all hatch from eggs
928. Deck
929. True
930. 80 days
931. Purple
932. Ducks
933. Latin
934. Static electricity
935. Tug-of-war
936. New Zealand
937. Japanese poem
938. Four teeth
939. Salsa
940. Sherwood forest
941. Merlin
942. Bugle

943. Cirrus
944. Cricket
945. Swan
946. His plane
947. Adamantium
948. Microscope
949. A Christmas Carol
950. Insects
951. Penguins
952. Rip Van Winkle
953. Polynesia the parrot
954. Moaning Myrtle
955. Horse
956. Round
957. Andy
958. False
959. Urban
960. Eight
961. New York City
962. Cybermen
963. Sculpture
964. Bigger
965. Panda
966. B
967. Ancient Greece
968. Turkey
969. Winnie the Pooh
970. Ice hockey
971. Spanish
972. True
973. Lily
974. The Beatles
975. Electric guitar
976. Mice
977. Venus

978. Guinea pig
979. 300 runs
980. Euro
981. Beatrix Potter
982. Starfish
983. Putter
984. Eighth month
985. Africa
986. Woolly mammoth
987. Wear it
988. False
989. Water
990. Eggs
991. Europe
992. Sunglasses
993. 27 years
994. True
995. Portugal
996. Ganges
997. Diagonally
998. Paint
999. Gallop
1000. South Pole